PARENTING WITHOUT PROSECCO

By Suzanne Davison

Welcome to
Parenting Without Prosecco

Hi

I am Suzanne Davison, business owner, family Coach, mum to Molly and Amy and two dogs, wife to Mark and somewhere amongst the midst of these people I'm Me.

Life is stressful these days and often those stresses end up inside the family home making it difficult to communicate, understand each other and function as the family you set out to have. Mother Nature is clever as if we knew beforehand what it would really be like I'd suggest the population would be smaller, hence why there was no hand book when you had your kids.

I wrote this little book in honour of parents who are doing their best but are open to learn how to do it even better. This book is full of tips that I've picked up through my training, clients I've worked with and things my family have taught me over the years. There are affirmations that help you trust you are doing ok and funny bits to keep a smile on your face but the main thing I want this book to do is to let you know you aren't on your own, there's an even bigger family out here that has got you and I'd love you to join it.

I've had a rollercoaster journey as a wife and parent and there were times I thought someone is going to have to leave to the house but luckily we navigated the waters and made it through. I do wish I'd had these tips when my kids were young as I may not have drunk my body weight in Prosecco ☺

I hope you enjoy the book and I'd love to hear any tips you have that I can pass on by you sharing them on Facebook group https://www.facebook.com/groups/FixMyFamily/

I raise a glass to all mums and dads and especially to my family whom without, I wouldn't be where I am today.

Tons of love to you all

Suzanne xx

P.S. Don't forget to grab your FREE 'Parenting Without Prosecco' Masterclass at www.FixmyFamily.co.uk

5

TIP

As parents you are creating your children's emotional foundation that the rest of their lives will be built upon. To make a strong one they have three fundamental needs 1. Love and connection 2. Security, feeling safe physically and emotionally 3. Significance, feeling that they are special and worthy of attention and that they are good enough.

6

AFFIRMATION

Everything thing I do serves a
purpose for my family.

FUNNY BIT

Based on the amount of laundry, I'm going to assume that there are people living here that I've never seen.

8

TIP

Love is a confusing word as it is based on the definition of the person saying it. I can say I love you and buy you a bunch of flowers but I could also say I love and give you a bunch of fives. Make sure your family has a clear definition of what love is and you all stick to it. Children get very confused when parents love them in a different way example one parent is warm and nurturing the other is aggressive and cold. This confusion will affect your child's relationships, their self-esteem and the way they treat people.

9

TIP

Mind your language – you are your children's biggest teachers. Remember the way you speak to people. Subconsciously, you are saying to the child that it is ok. If you don't want your kids to swear then don't swear yourself. If you don't want your kids to be mean to other people, don't let them hear their parents being mean.

10

AFFIRMATION

You are the exact parent your
child needs to learn important
life lessons.

FUNNY BIT

Ever had a job where you had no experience, no training, you weren't allowed to quit and people's lives were at stake? That's parenting

12

TIP

Your children will model themselves
on one of their parents more than
the other. Make sure if they are
modelling you, you are a role model.

13

AFFIRMATION

There is peace and love in my home, even in the midst of chaos.

FUNNY BIT

If I ever go missing, please follow my kids. They can find me no matter where I try to hide.

15

TIP

If your child is behaving in a way that you don't like, don't punish the behaviour look underneath it. Why are they behaving that way? Are they stressed, upset, wanting attention? Take time to understand your child.

16

AFFIRMATION

Loving my children is more
important than loving every
moment of parenthood.

FUNNY BIT

How I managed to keep my children alive but killed every house plant I've ever owned is a mystery.

18

TIP

Think.. "Do I want my children to have the same relationships that I have?" If not, change them now so they don't copy you.

19

AFFIRMATION

Kids aren't little warriors who are out to get me, they are little humans who need to be nurtured.

FUNNY BIT

When my kids become wild and
unruly, I use a soft playpen.
When they are finished, I climb
out.

21

TIP

Let them make a mistake, that's how we learn. Rather than get mad, talk through other options they have so they learn. Your child spills milk, show him how to pour the milk so he doesn't do it again rather than just telling him off.

AFFIRMATION

My child is the perfect teacher for me, and I'm learning so much.

FUNNY BIT

Recipe for iced coffee – have kids, make coffee, forget you made coffee, drink it cold.

24

TIP

If you want a teenager to naturally tidy their bedroom train them when they are young but make it FUN, the brain will keep doing things that make it feel good.

25

AFFIRMATION

My love and connection helps
my child above all else.

FUNNY BIT

Before becoming a parent, I didn't know I could ruin someone's life by simply asking them to clean their teeth..

27

TIP

Do not expect your child to suddenly have life skills just because they have turned a certain age, they need to be taught life skills to know how to handle situations, you can help them learn do this.

AFFIRMATION

My children are strong, safe and
supported.

FUNNY BIT

The quickest way for a parent
to get the attention of their
child is to sit down and look
comfortable.

30

TIP

Do not expect your kids to know how lucky they are compared to you when you were a child. They can only compare themselves to what they have and people around them.

AFFIRMATION

I am the exact parent my child needs to blossom so I don't need to compare myself to others.

FUNNY BIT

Then I thought to myself..
"What is the point of cleaning if
my family are going to continue
to live here?"

33

TIP

If you want your child to have good values around money YOU have to instil this in them. Make them earn things, and then they will look after them and appreciate them. Just buying your child something does not make them appreciate money.

34

AFFIRMATION

I am worthy of the love I
receive from my family.

35

FUNNY BIT

Friend: "What's parenting like?"
ME: "You know all the side
effects they list on prescription
drugs? It's like that".

36

TIP

Don't clip your child's wings. Your child's mission in life is to gain independence. So, when she's developmentally capable of putting her toys away, clearing her plate from the table, and dressing herself, let her. Giving a child responsibility young is good for her self-esteem (and your sanity!).

37

AFFIRMATION

Giving my child time and attention is more important than giving them material things.

38

FUNNY BIT

Both of you can't look good at the same time – its either me or the house.

39

TIP

If your child is finding school stressful understand why. If they find it hard to concentrate, are too chatty, fidgety, can't get their work started or finished, forgetful, get confused, angry or socially these are possible signs of learning challenges that can get punished rather than supported.

AFFIRMATION

Take care of your body it is the
only place you have to live

FUNNY BIT

When I say to my child "get dressed". Their interpretation is "stand around naked watching television with one sock on".

42

TIP

LISTEN to what your child says, do not shut them down, do not tell them they are wrong, calmly listen to what they say and show interest to understand. If you do this with the small stuff then as they get older, they will tell you the big stuff.

43

AFFIRMATION

Taking care of myself is a
responsibility I will model to my
children without guilt.

44

TIP

Your child's self-esteem is created by the environment that surrounds them. Your child is looking for its outside world to approve of who they are. You can't control other children or teachers but you can make sure that their home is always the place they come to feel good. Do not criticise your child if they do something wrong, help them to understand what they could have done better. Feedback only.

45

FUNNY BIT

My daughter woke up at 6:06am today instead of her normal 6:00am because we let her stay up 5 hours past her bedtime last night.

46

TIP

CONSISTANT parenting is less confusing for children. When one parent says no and the other says yes, one confused child. If one parent is positive and tells them they love them and the other is grumpy and doesn't say anything, one confused child. If one parent spends lots of time with the child and the other doesn't, one confused child. This will affect your child's self-esteem.

47

AFFIRMATION

Today I will find peace in being good enough because perfection is impossible.

48

FUNNY BIT

Becoming a mother makes you
realise you can do almost
anything one handed.

49

TIP

If the parents are split up make sure that both homes are a positive experience for the child. Remember it is not their fault your relationship didn't work and a child should NEVER feel sorry for the hurt party as this will affect their mental health.

50

AFFIRMATION

It's ok to need and want a
break from my family. It's ok to
take that break!

51

FUNNY BIT

When I tell my kids I'll do something in a minute, what I'm really saying is "please forget".

TIP

If parents are split up make sure the
child understands why this happened.
Do not brush it under the carpet, they
deserve to fully understand why they
aren't together. With young kids, you
can draw it out as a story for them,
teenagers can be spoken to in a more
grown up way. Do not make it a taboo
subject as they will need to learn from
this or it will affect their future
relationships.

53

AFFIRMATION

Establishing personal boundaries and sticking to them helps me remember that I am important too.

54

TIP

If a child has been bereaved make sure they have found a belief around death that makes them feel comfortable. A child that doesn't can often become more anxious and worried.

55

AFFIRMATION

Rather than simply reacting, I will choose my next behaviour.

FUNNY BIT

It's like no one in my family appreciates the fact that I stayed up all night overthinking for them.

57

TIP

If your child has anxiety or depression do not expect them to one day just snap out of it. If they can't open up to you, don't take it personally, seek professional help as soon as you notice it. Don't leave it hoping they'll grow out of it.

58

AFFIRMATION

I understand that my child is a separate individual and I give him enough space for his individuality.

59

FUNNY BIT

Having one child makes you a parent, having two makes you a referee.

60

TIP

When we are stressed we have three options – get angry, worry/panic or cry. To help your child manage these feelings, teach them relaxation techniques from a young age, this will help them manage stress as they get older. Meditation is excellent with adults and kids as it can be done at home.

61

AFFIRMATION

This moment will not last
forever.

FUNNY BIT

One day I'll be thankful that my kid is strong willed, but that will not be today, not in this supermarket..

63

TIP

If you want your child to grow up being honest with you, then do not react angrily if they say something you don't like. Talk to them about it and explain why you aren't happy. If you just shout, your child will not tell you anything.

64

AFFIRMATION

As everything swirls by me, I
tune in and listen to my breath.

65

FUNNY BIT

I hate it when my parents won't let me go anywhere then moan that I'm always on my computer.

66

TIP

Pick your battles or it's a bloody long war. Decide between both parents what are the boundaries around behaviour, bedtime, use of internet, homework, chores around the house etc., and think about which are the most important rules to be followed and you both stick to them rigidly.

67

AFFIRMATION

I am stronger than the problem

FUNNY BIT

My kid is turning out to be just like me – well played karma, well played.

69

TIP

Having a visual set of rules up in the house gives a clear message to everyone about what is expected. Do not move the goalpost unless you have sat down with them and explained why they've moved. If parents have split, make sure both houses support these rules.

AFFIRMATION

I do not need to be in control
as I trust that everything is
happening for a reason, I
choose to relax and breathe.

FUNNY BIT

Motherhood - when 90% of
your time is putting other
people's crap away.

72

TIP

Quality not quantity. Children want quality time with their parents. It doesn't have to be hours, but it does have to be quality. So not on your phone or emails, be present.

73

AFFIRMATION

My children are not me; they are their own separate and beautiful beings.

FUNNY BIT

I always thought I'd be a
patient mum and then I
watched my son try to zip his
own jacket.

75

TIP

Do not try and fix your child by what you think, ask them what they need from you to make them feel better and meet that need.

AFFIRMATIONS

I am doing the best I can. I am enough.

FUNNY BIT

You can be a mess and still be
a good parent we are allowed
to be both.

78

TIP

Remember if your child is on the phone a lot, it is often because they are talking to their friends. Their world is very different to the one you grew up in, do not expect them to behave the way you did when you were younger.

AFFIRMATION

I am here in the present
moment, with kindness and
curiosity.

FUNNY BIT

Don't be so hard on yourself,
the mum in ET had an alien
living in her house for days and
didn't even notice.

81

TIP

If you have Xbox or Play Station, set clear boundaries around how much time they have on it but remember if they are in the middle of a game with friends, it is hard to walk away so may need some gentle coaxing. If you want them to come off, entice them with something they can do with you, not just come off and do nothing.

82

AFFIRMATION

I am the most important
teacher in my children's lives.

83

FUNNY BIT

Silence is golden – unless you have a toddler then its suspicious.

84

TIP

Don't let kids do gaming just before bed as it will turn into a battle and their brains will be too stimulated to sleep. Give them 30-60 mins of restful time before they go to bed.

85

TIP

If you don't want your child to have anxiety, make sure you let them do stuff without you having to tell them of all the dangers that could happen. Your child needs to believe they can keep themselves safe.

86

AFFIRMATION

I love my child, especially when
we differ.

FUNNY BIT

All of us have moments in our lives that test our courage. Taking children into a house with a white carpet is one of them.

TIP

If your child has low confidence
make sure they don't hear you say it,
"Oh Johnny isn't very confident" for
example. This will reinforce a limiting
belief that will be harder for them to
overcome. Remember a child will
believe what they are told.

89

AFFIRMATION

I trust my intuition. I am willing
to listen to that still, small
voice within.

FUNNY BIT

I like to put cute little notes in my kids lunch boxes like, "I love you", "I know what you did", "thanks for the stretch marks".

91

TIP

To help your child's self-esteem, ask them to tell you about all the times they have felt confident. Write it up on a chart and list out all the skills they have and every night get them to read it out with an "I" statement. "I am very good at football", "I am very kind", "I am very clever", "I feel confident when I'm.."

92

AFFIRMATION

I am so very proud of my children.

FUNNY BIT

People who say they sleep like a baby probably don't have them.

94

TIP

If your child is having social issues and is taking things personally draw out the different people involved and see if you can help get your child to see the situation from all the different perspectives. It doesn't mean they have to agree with the behaviour, but it opens them up to other ways to look at a situation.

95

AFFIRMATION

I balance my life between work,
rest, and play.

FUNNY BIT

Some days I do yoga and don't
yell at the kid's other days I
scream at the kids while eating
cake it's called balance.

97

TIP

If someone has been unkind to your child tell them not to take it personally and explain that no one has taught that child how to be as kind as them.

98

AFFIRMATION

I give my children positive
support whenever they need it.

FUNNY BIT

Somewhere along the way, I
became a person who answers
"yes" to the question "can I put
my dirty tissue in your pocket?"

TIP

Teach your child to ask WHY. If someone is treating them badly get them to ask the person why they would want to upset them or why would they say mean things as it makes them not a kind person. The same applies for a child to be able to question a parent, "Mum why do you have to shout at me it makes me feel bad. Why can't you just talk to me calmly?".

AFFIRMATION

I love my family members just
as they are. I do not try to
change anyone.

FUNNY BIT

Hi I am a parent and my hobbies are making food that no one eats and counting to 3. I enjoy long walks to the bathroom by myself and the rare moment when I get to watch a show that isn't animated. I also love wine, I really love wine..

103

TIP

Manage your own stress. Often, we bring stresses in from outside the home that make us irritable or upset. This leads to us behaving in a negative way towards our family, and yet it is not their fault if you have a bad day at work, or your mum annoyed you today. If everyone is bringing into the home external stress, it makes it very hard to have a relaxed calm home. Find a way to release your stress before you come home or as quickly as possible when you are in. Spending 10 minutes meditating can bring you back that equilibrium.

104

AFFIRMATION

Life is a book full of chapters,
each one will be over and I will
learn from the experience.

FUNNY BIT

When my kids act up in public, I love shouting "just wait until I tell your mum!" and pretend they're not mine.

TIP

If you and your partner are not happy
DO NOT stay like it, do something
about it however hard. Your children
are learning from you what love is, if
they see someone treating the other
badly they will either find someone
that treats them badly or they will
treat their partner badly.

107

AFFIRMATION

Everything turns out ok in the
end and if it isn't ok then it isn't
the end

FUNNY BIT

"Oooh – everyone's ready and there's so much time before we have to leave the house so I'll relax and enjoy a hot cuppa before we leave.." said no parent, ever.

109

TIP

Family meetings are an excellent way to open up communication and talk about the things that maybe niggling you and family members. Rather than letting stress build up until you explode, often over something silly, talk about things when you are calm. Start this when kids are young and it won't be odd to them when they are older. It will take you to mediate the meeting, so not to allow it to turn into a row.

110

AFFIRMATION

I will let go of how I think
today is supposed to go, and
accept how it imperfectly
happens.

111

FUNNY BIT

People who claim the most
beautiful thing is to see their
children sleep haven't watched
their kids do the dishes.

TIP

If you or the other parent has mental health conditions such as anxiety or depression, get help first and talk to your children about it. Hiding it doesn't stop them from learning it or suffering for it if you aren't able to parent as effectively as you would like to. It also shows that it's good to talk when you don't feel happy.

113

AFFIRMATION

You are doing the best with
what you have.

FUNNY BIT

Never in the entire history of calming down has anyone ever calmed down by being told to calm down.

115

TIP

Are you a "never enough parent" –
telling your child they have done a
good job but then follow it by "BUT if
you did this it could be better". Your
child will learn they are never good
enough – as parents just let them be
enough.

116

AFFIRMATION

A successful relationship with
my child is not defined by what
we have but by the time we
spent together.

FUNNY BIT

A perfect metaphor for parenting to stand up in a hammock without spilling your wine.

118

TIP

Always cuddle your children and they
will be comfortable with cuddles
when they are an adult.

119

AFFIRMATION

Family we may not have it all together but together we have it all.

FUNNY BIT

I start off each day as Mary Poppins and end it as Cruella De Vil.

121

TIP

If yelling at your child to tidy their
bedroom doesn't work, think of a new
strategy or just keep the door closed.

122

AFFIRMATION

Our home is a safe and
peaceful haven.

123

FUNNY BIT

Parenting is a lot like the bar scene: everyone's sticky, it's the same music over and over again and occasionally someone pukes.

124

TIP

Do not be a helicopter parent hovering over your children waiting to swoon down and rescue them from danger, trust your child can make good decisions and will call you if needed.

125

AFFIRMATION

Today I am at peace.

126

FUNNY BIT

No one is full of more false
hope than a parent bringing a
chair to the beach.

127

TIP

The house doesn't have to be clean and tidy to be happy. If YOU have a problem with mess and dirt learn to relax around it by focussing on the fun that you have whilst making a mess.

AFFIRMATION

I might not see it now, but the
time I'm investing does matter.

FUNNY BIT

Every time I say "no" my kids hear, "ask again, she didn't understand the question".

130

TIP

Do not compare your child's progress or ability to other children; they will make it in their own time, in their own way.

131

AFFIRMATION

Life is good, and so it is!

FUNNY BIT

You know that you are a parent when your instinct is to catch puke with your bare hands.

133

TIP

Teach your child gratitude by each night asking them to name 5 things they are grateful for. It makes them look for the positives in life.

134

AFFIRMATION

We are all here to learn grow
and share. I am in a learning
phase, soon to grow and then
to share.

FUNNY BIT

As a parent, there's a lot more yelling at people from the bathroom than I would've imagined.

136

TIP

Your child's education is not as important as their mental health; make sure they get a healthy balance going through their school life with hobbies, friends, family time and studies.

137

TIP

Tell your child that there is a bright
future for them whatever their
learning ability is. Some kids just can't
shine in school.

138

AFFIRMATION

I love and respect my child as much as I love and respect myself.

FUNNY BITS

Bedtime – when suddenly kids
are hungry, thirsty and have an
important question to ask.

140

TIP

Children need positive attention. If they do not receive positive attention from family, they may choose to seek out negative attention. This is because negative attention is still attention, and any attention is better than being ignored.

141

TIP

If you find yourself drinking to be able to deal with the stress, find a more powerful alternative exercise or meditation are great ones. You can teach this to your child as well so they will follow suit when they get older.

142

AFFIRMATION

In our greatest pain we tap into our deepest power, you've got this!

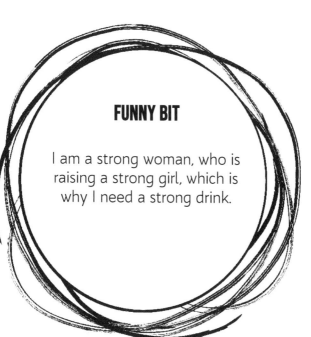

FUNNY BIT

I am a strong woman, who is raising a strong girl, which is why I need a strong drink.

144

TIP

If your child has mental health issues, relax they will come through it. You asking lots of questions about how they feel can add to their stress so remember just listen, do not try and fix unless they ask for it. Keep your home relaxed as it is key to have one environment where they are able to relax more.

145

TIP

Teach your kids healthy behaviour around social media. Make sure you follow their accounts, be aware they can have more than one account. Do not let them spend all their time looking at other people's lives, help them to make sure they are creating a good life for themselves.

AFFIRMATION

My children don't want perfect,
they want me.

FUNNY BIT

Parenting was much easier when I was raising my non-existent kids, hypothetically.

148

TIP

Family time is so important to keeping your kids wanting to be with you. Have a family bucket list that you all compile and every couple of weeks do something off the list, take turns choosing but you may have to arrange it.

AFFIRMATION

All is well in my world.
Everything is working out for
my highest good. Out of this
situation only good will come. I
am safe!

FUNNY BIT

A body like this doesn't happen
overnight it takes pregnancy,
some neglect and additional
slices of pizza.

151

TIP

Don't compare siblings. If a child thinks his or her brother or sister is favoured, it can create a rivalry that may last the rest of their lives and cause problems in your family. Make sure your kids know that they are loved equally.

TIP

To bring up independent children
that make good decisions, allow
them to make their own decisions.
Rather than always telling them what
they should be doing, get them to
think about the situation first and tell
you what they think they should do,
discuss if necessary.

153

AFFIRMATION

I am confident and growing in
my parenting role.

FUNNY BIT

Yay.. it's Friday night..oh wait
we are parents..

TIP

Think about your parents and write a list of everything they did well and make sure you are doing that, and then write a list of what they didn't do well and check in with yourself to make sure you are not repeating that behaviour.

156

AFFIRMATION

I trust the process of life.

157

FUNNY BIT

When you fake sleep to help
your child sleep, then you wake
from a 4 hour nap.

158

TIP

Give them space - We all need time for ourselves. Teenagers need their own space, time for themselves and the right not to tell their parents everything about their lives. Respect your teenager's right to privacy and try to remember what it was like to be a teenager.

159

AFFIRMATION

There is peace and love in my home, even in the midst of chaos.

160

FUNNY BIT

I'm just a mum, standing in front of my partner, trying to say something that I can no longer remember because our kids interrupted us 175 times.

161

TIP

Be careful if your work is busy and stressful that it doesn't take over your home life too. Kids need you to be at home when you are there, they are only young once.

162

AFFIRMATION

Filling my mind with pleasant thoughts is the quickest road to health.

FUNNY BIT

I want my children to be independent head strong people, just not while I'm raising them.

164

TIP

Don't be an invisible parent. If you want a close relationship with your children when they are older put the time and effort in when they are young.

165

AFFIRMATION

I am grateful for the time with
my kids today.

FUNNY BIT

That awkward moment when
you're not sure if you actually
have some free time or if
you've forgotten what you have
to do.

167

TIP

If your child has anxiety, don't push them to do big things, break everything down into small goals so they get some quick wins. Get them to write their worries out and ask what is the worst that can happen, get them to come up with a solution to how they can handle this, then ask what is the most likely thing to happen then finally ask, what is the best thing to happen. It helps your child from catastrophising the situation.

AFFIRMATION

Just as the needs of my
children matter, so do my own.

FUNNY BIT

I used to have functioning brain
cells but I traded them for
children.

170

TIP

Don't expect teenagers to agree with everything you say. The teenage years are a time of testing opinions and people. Sometimes parents and teenagers have to agree to differ. Your teenager is more likely to respect your views if you respect theirs.

171

AFFIRMATION

Today I will love fiercely, laugh freely and live courageously. I can never get today back.

FUNNY BITS

I just spent twenty minutes
helping my child search for
their chocolate I ate last night..

173

TIP

If your child gets worried do not shut their worries down. Listen to their worries and get them to work out a plan if it were to happen. I'm worried that Mary doesn't like me today and won't play with me. Go through all the options they can do if Mary doesn't play with them.

174

AFFIRMATION

Parenting. The days are long
but the years are short.

FUNNY BIT

They say women speak 20,000 words a day, I have a daughter that gets that done by breakfast.

176

TIP

Accept that life changes when you have a child. Lazy Saturday mornings in bed are replaced by football matches and dance. Remember, you still need to make time for each other – date nights and weekend getaways are important for your relationship.

AFFIRMATION

One bad day does not make
me a bad parent. One bad day
makes me human.

FUNNY BIT

You know you're a mum when..
you understand why mummy
bear's porridge was cold.

179

TIP

Don't be a mother or a father. Be a
parent – work together as a team
and don't be a martyr. Work out roles
and responsibilities so you don't feel
resentful of the other, instead you
manage your expectations so you
don't get let down.

TIP

Don't try to make your child your friend. This does not mean you have to be their enemy. You are their friend (and greatest advocate and supporter). But they are not *your* friend. Children aren't stupid. Who wants to be friends with the most excruciatingly embarrassing person ever? That person is you.

181

AFFIRMATION

I am what my child needs.
Worrying about what others
think only distracts me from
being the parent I need to be.

182

FUNNY BIT

Does going to the loo without
an audience count as 'me time'?

TIP

Just say "No". Resist the urge to take
on extra obligations at the office or
become the Volunteer Queen at your
child's school. You will never, ever
regret spending more time with your
children. The best way to be involved
in your kid's life is to be in it.

184

AFFIRMATION

I trust my intuition to make intentional parenting choices and decisions.

185

FUNNY BIT

Wake up extra early so that you and your kids can still be 20 minutes late wherever you go.

186

TIP

Teach kids this bravery trick. Tell them to always notice the colour of a person's eyes. Making eye contact will help a hesitant child appear more confident and will help any kid to be more assertive and less likely to be picked on.

187

AFFIRMATION

I will push through challenges
so that my struggles today will
become my strengths
tomorrow.

FUNNY BIT

I finally had the talk with my kids I told them that the animals in the wild eat their young so they'd better get their shit together.

189

TIP

Fess up when you blow it. This is the best way to show your child how and when she should apologise.

190

AFFIRMATION

I will let go of how I think today is supposed to go and accept how it imperfectly happens.

191

FUNNY BIT

When your children are
teenagers, it's important to
have a dog so that someone in
the house is happy to see you.

192

TIP

Gossip about your kids. Fact: What we overhear is far more potent than what we are told directly. Make praise more effective by letting your child "catch" you whispering a compliment about him to Nan, Dad, or even his teddy.

193

AFFIRMATION

I forgive myself for being an imperfect parent. Today I will let go of the guilt weighing on my shoulders.

194

FUNNY BITS

My idea of getting lucky is
having someone else do the
laundry.

195

TIP

Explain to your kids why values are important. The simple answer: When you're kind, generous, honest, and respectful, you make the people around you feel good. More important, you feel good about yourself.

196

AFFIRMATION

I am brave and courageous for trying even when I think I can't do it.

197

FUNNY BIT

You know when life has changed when going to the supermarket by yourself is a vacation.

198

TIP

Don't make your child a 'people pleaser' whereby they are more bothered about keeping everyone else happy rather than doing what makes them happy. Allow them to have a voice and give their opinion.

199

AFFIRMATION

I give myself permission to do
something to nurture ME.

200

FUNNYBIT

Great parenting lies somewhere between "don't do that" and "ah, what the hell".

201

TIP

Say "I love you" whenever you feel it,
even if it's 743 times a day. You
simply cannot spoil a child with too
many mushy words of affection and
too many smooches. Not possible.

202

AFFIRMATION

I accept where I am in life and
will make the most of today.

203

FUNNY BIT

So I stepped away for 2
seconds..the beginning of every
parenting horror story.

TIP

Don't raise a spoiled kid. Keep this
thought in mind: Every child is a
treasure, but no child is the centre of
the universe. Teach them accordingly
or they will struggle socially.

205

AFFIRMATION

Everything is exactly the way it
needs to be in order to learn
the lessons I need the most.

FUNNY BIT

Parenting is saying the same thing over and over but expecting a different result. Oddly enough, that is the definition of insanity.. a coincidence.. I think not.

207

TIP

Keep the TV in the family room.
Research has repeatedly shown that
children with a TV in their bedroom
weigh more, sleep less, and have
lower grades and poorer social skills.
Also parents with a television in their
bedroom have sex less often.

208

AFFIRMATION

In the eyes, mind and heart of
my child, I am a good parent.

FUNNY BIT

My friend asked me recently
"what's the most difficult part of
being a parent?" Without a
shadow of a doubt "it's the
kids!" I replied.

210

TIP

Keep in mind what grandmas always say. Children are not yours, they are only lent to you for a time. In those fleeting years, do your best to help them grow up to be good people.

211

AFFIRMATIONS

Taking care of myself makes
me a better parent because I
parent from abundance, not
from lack thereof.

212

FUNNY BIT

Nothing good comes from a conversation that begins with "hey mum, are you in a good mood?"

213

TIP

Savour the moments. Yes, parenthood is the most exhausting job on the planet. Yes, your house is a mess, the laundry's piled up, and the dog needs to be walked. But your kid just laughed. Enjoy it now - it will be over far too fast.

ABOUT THE AUTHOR

Suzanne has over 10 years' experience working within the complementary therapy sector. She is a qualified clinical hypnotherapist, NLP practitioner, Life and Business Coach. She has helped thousands of teenagers and families navigate their way through the trials and tribulations and unexpected trauma of family and school life.

She has 2 teenage daughters one who herself has struggled with severe depression, anxiety and ADD the other who has ADHD just like her mother!

215

She is a leading facilitator, speaker, and therapist who is passionate about helping as many families learn how to deal and manage with life's stresses to create a happy and healthy home.

Her flourishing practice is based in Essex where she is launching her Fix My Family training programme so more families can be supported.

Get Your Bonus Parenting Without Prosecco Masterclass at

www.FixmyFamily.co.uk

216

Printed in Great Britain
by Amazon